DISCOVER

BLACK BEARS

By
Margaret Anderson
Nancy Field
Karen Stephenson

Illustrated by Michael Maydak

Computer design and several illustrations by Betsy True

Produced in cooperation with the North American Bear Center

Dog-Eared Publications acknowledges the use of photographs by Lynn Rogers Ph.D, Maggie Heino, Kim Sager, Ian McAllister and Richard Johnson in the creation of the illustrations in this book.

 Educators, please refer to inside back cover. Send correspondence to Dog-Eared Publications LLC, P.O. Box 620863, Middleton, WI 53562-0863; Web Site: http://www.dog-eared.com

ISBN 0-941042-37-5 (10 digit)
ISBN 978-0-941042-37-6 (13 digit)

Printed in the USA

Have You Ever Wondered?

The three biologists crouched in the snow close to the bear's den. They could hear the signal from the radio collar of a female bear. They had put on the collar two years ago. How was she doing? Had she grown? Was she alone in the den or did she have cubs?

Maggie, one of the team members, crawled into the hole. She had her jabstick ready. Taking aim, she injected the bear with a drug that would make the animal sleep while the biologists examined her. Once the drug had taken effect, the others dragged the bear out into the open. They cheered when Maggie crawled out holding two tiny, squalling cubs. She stuffed them inside her coat to keep them warm.

The group set to work. They measured the bear's length and girth, her neck and her paws. They gave her a new collar with a fresh battery. Next they weighed her. Weighing a 200-pound sleeping bear isn't easy. But the cubs were no problem. Maggie placed a cub in her wool hat and hung it from a spring scale. It weighed just over 4 pounds. After the mother had been dragged back into her den, Maggie crawled in and placed the cubs beside her. They were none the worse for their adventure.

Crawling into a bear den doesn't sound like a good idea – even if you're sure the bear is sleeping. For trained scientists, it is safe. By getting to know bears up close, they have learned a great deal about them. We now know that black bears are basically shy animals that try to avoid danger while they roam in the forests looking for food.

Bears and people have a lot in common. Both are very smart animals. Although bears mostly walk on four feet, they can walk upright on two feet. Like us, they have five toes, but instead of nails, they have long claws that help them climb trees and tear logs apart. We would have trouble holding onto a tree with our fingernails. The American black bear is not a ferocious animal – but it's not a cuddly teddy bear, either! To learn more about black bears, track them through the pages of your discovery book.

Maggie Heino

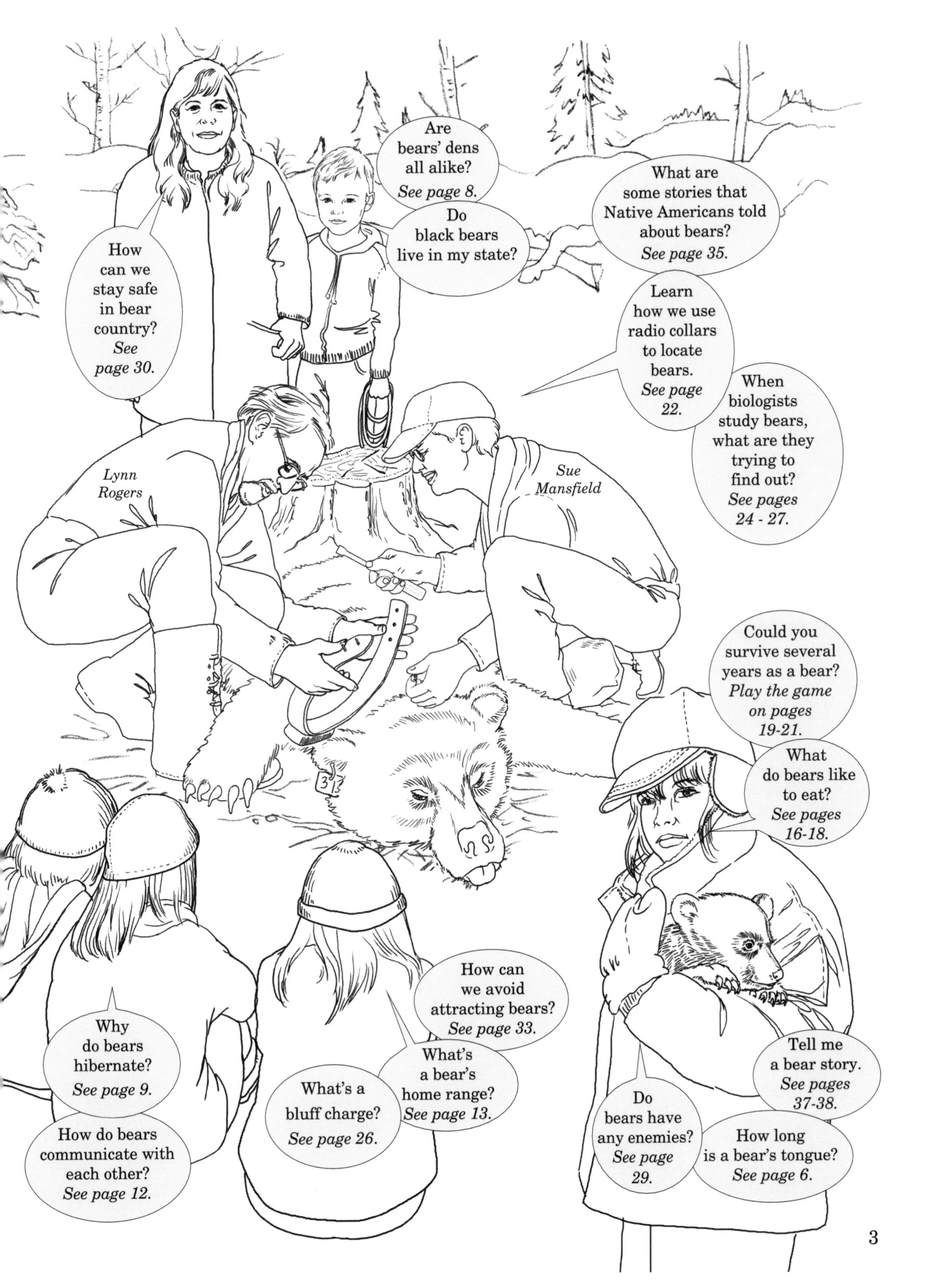
How can we stay safe in bear country? See page 30.
Are bears' dens all alike? See page 8.
Do black bears live in my state?
What are some stories that Native Americans told about bears? See page 35.
Learn how we use radio collars to locate bears. See page 22.
When biologists study bears, what are they trying to find out? See pages 24 - 27.
Lynn Rogers
Sue Mansfield
Could you survive several years as a bear? Play the game on pages 19-21.
What do bears like to eat? See pages 16-18.
3
How can we avoid attracting bears? See page 33.
Why do bears hibernate? See page 9.
How do bears communicate with each other? See page 12.
What's a bluff charge? See page 26.
What's a bear's home range? See page 13.
Do bears have any enemies? See page 29.
Tell me a bear story. See pages 37-38.
How long is a bear's tongue? See page 6.

Meet our Three Bears

Of the eight **species** (kinds) of bears found around the world, three of these live in North America. They are the American black bear, the brown bear, and the polar bear. Their scientific names are *Ursus americanus*, *Ursus arctos*, and *Ursus maritimus*. *Ursus* and *maritimus* are Latin words meaning "bear" and "sea." *Arctos* is Greek for "bear."

Most **American black bears** are black with a brown nose. Some have a white patch of fur on their chest. However, black bears can be brown, cinnamon, blue gray, or even white. They like forested areas where they can find their favorite foods — plants, nuts, berries and grubs.

Brown bears include the Kodiak bear and the grizzly bear. The Kodiak bear is only found on Kodiak Island in Alaska. The grizzly gets its name from the silvery-tipped hairs on the dark coat of older bears. Grizzlies like bushy, open country. Their long claws are good for digging up roots and small mammals.

The **polar bear** is found in the Arctic amid the snow and ice. It has a beautiful, yellowish-white coat. Its Latin name, meaning sea bear, fits it well. It spends much of its time in or near the ocean, where it hunts seals.

Grizzly or Black Bear?

Grizzly bears are fiercer than black bears. You can't tell them apart by their color. The grizzly bear isn't always brown; the black bear isn't always black. And size isn't a good clue, either. The average weight of a grizzly is 490 pounds (223 kg) compared with 220 lbs (100 kg) for a black bear. However, one male black bear weighed a record 880 pounds (400 kg).

Grizzly Bear

Found in Alaska and in northwestern states and western provinces.

Dished, or caved in, face when seen from the side.

Shoulder hump due to large muscles for digging.

Rarely climbs trees.

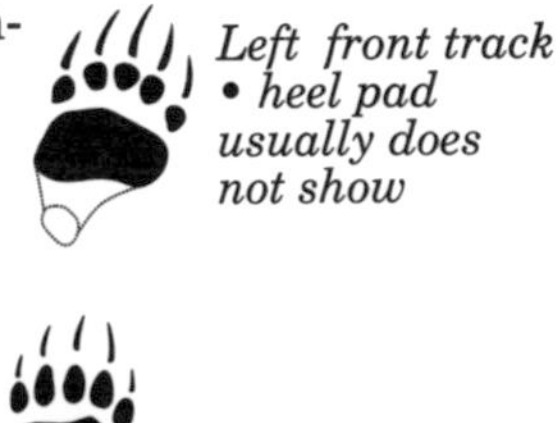

Black Bear

Widespread over Canada and found in 42 states, including Florida and Louisiana.

Face forms a straight line from its forehead to its nose.

No shoulder hump.

Good climber.

Left front track
• heel pad usually does not show
• toes more separated and arched

Left rear track

These wildlife photographs have lost their labels. Label them as "Grizzly" "Black Bear" or "can't tell."

1. ____________
2. ____________
3. ____________
4. ____________
5. ____________
6. ____________

Answers on last page

Black Bear - Up Close

A bear's body is designed to help it find food and to keep it safe. Its dense fur coat keeps it warm in the winter. After a bear emerges from its den in the spring, it needs food. It sniffs the air and picks up the scent of a rotting log. It tears the log apart with its strong claws and then scoops up some grubs with its long, sticky tongue. The shape of the bear's body parts often matches their function or job.

Ears Good hearing. Cubs' ears large compared with size of head.

Eyes Sees well at night and in daytime. Good close-up vision — food is mostly close to the ground.

Nose Excellent sense of smell helps find food and mates, identify cubs, and avoid humans. Can detect smells for up to 3 miles (4.8 km.) or more.

Lips Free from gums so they can twist to grasp tiny berries.

Tongue Can reach 6 inches out of the mouth as it picks up a grub.

Teeth Bears eat both plants and meat with their 42 teeth. The teeth help tear apart logs, biting out entire chunks. How are the teeth designed for different jobs?

Look at the skull. Which item fits in each space to the right?

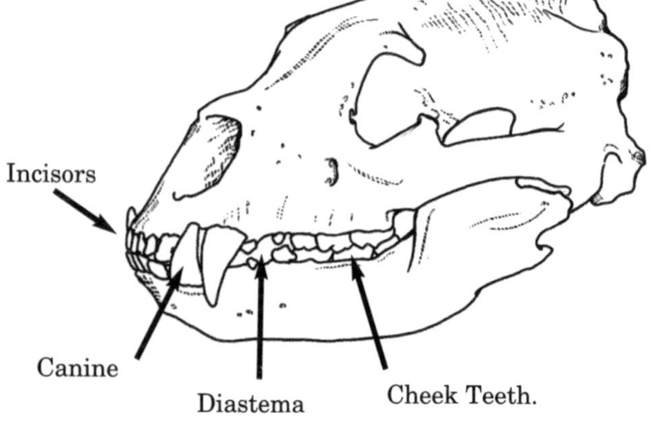

Large rounded ears

Eyes set close together

Flexible lips

Long, sticky tongue

Incisors

Canine

Diastema

Cheek Teeth.

1. ___________ for grinding and chewing plants.
2. ______________ for tearing wood apart.
3. The open area, or gap, where branches can be pulled through to strip leaves is the ________.
4. ______________ in the front of the mouth are used for chomping, nibbling, and tearing.

Fur Long guard hairs shed moisture and protect from dirt and insects. Dense, wooly underfur keeps the bear warm. Shed or molt their fur in spring or early summer. Get rid of this old hair by rubbing against trees and rocks.

Stomach Unchewed fruit is stored in the first part of the stomach and later moved to the second part. The second part uses pits from the fruit to grind up the food.

Illustrated from photo by Lynn Rogers

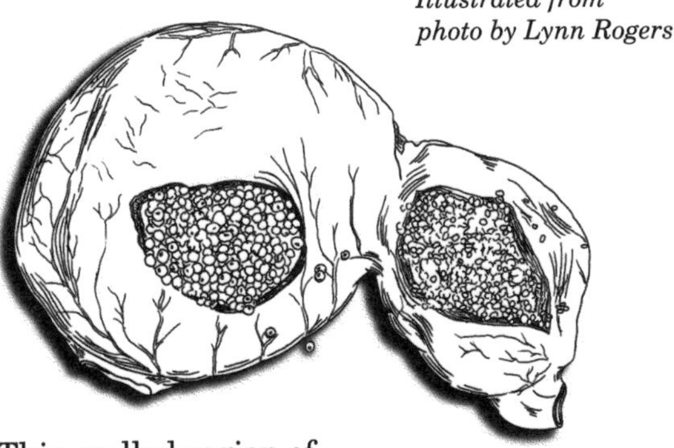

Thin-walled region of the stomach. Berries still whole.

Thick-walled region of the stomach. Acts like gizzard of a bird, grinding up food.

Body and muscles Built for strength rather than speed. Heavy shoulders and short back give strength and power.

Feet Walks with whole surface of paw on ground. Usually walk on four feet, but can (like humans) stand and even walk on two. Bears shed their foot pads over the winter.

Two inch long claws.

Claws Black or grayish brown and non-retractile (can't hide them the way a cat does). For climbing trees, digging, and raking up bedding. Black bears have the more tightly curved claws for climbing; grizzlies have longer, blunter claws for digging.

Describe the bear's body parts best suited for the following jobs.

1. Scooping up ants ______________
2. Finding food close to the ground ______________
3. Digging into wood ______________
4. Stripping leaves from branches ______________
5. Finding distant food ______________
6. Grinding food ______________
7. Climbing ______________
8. Grasping berries ______________
9. Sensing danger ______________

Answers on last page

The Long Sleep

Before the first snow falls, most black bears have chosen a den where they will sleep away the cold months. Bears find a different home each winter. Some use ready-made dens, like caves; others make a new den. A bear can move up to a ton of earth and rocks while digging its hole. The tunnel entrance is often well hidden. Sometimes the bear digs a den under a tree so that its roots support the roof.

The adult male bear is called a **boar**. The female is a **sow**. Baby bears are **cubs**. The boar and sow do not share a den. Cubs stay with their mother through the first summer and through the next winter. They are on their own by the following winter.

Use the code to find out where some bears chose to spend the winter.
The answers might surprise you!

1	2	3	4	5	6	7	8	9	10	11	12	13	14	15	16	17	18	19	20	21	22	23	24	25	26
A	B	C	D	E	F	G	H	I	J	K	L	M	N	O	P	Q	R	S	T	U	V	W	X	Y	Z

1. 8 15 12 12 15 23 / 9 14 / 20 18 5 5

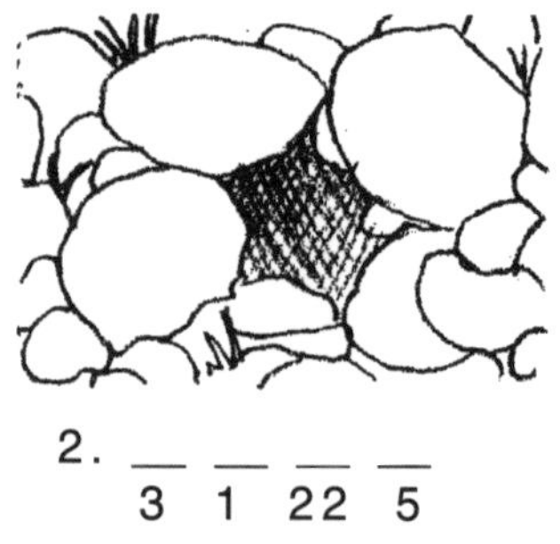

2. 3 1 22 5

3. 3 18 1 23 12 / 19 16 1 3 5

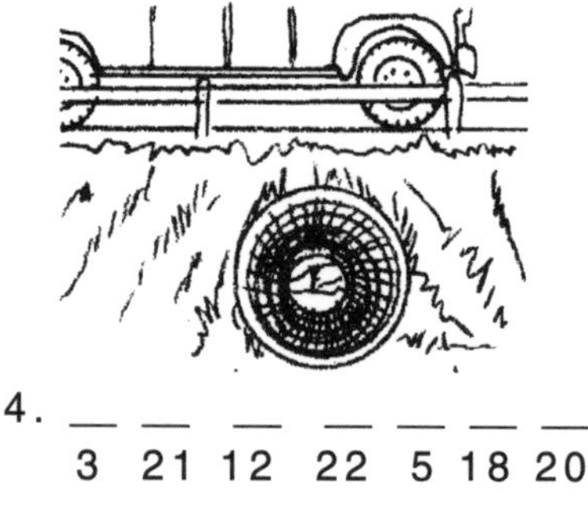

4. 3 21 12 22 5 18 20

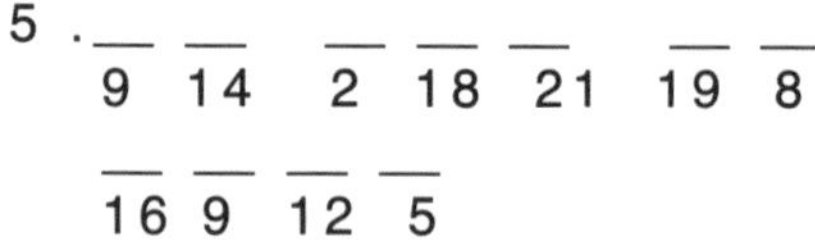

5. 9 14 / 2 18 21 19 8 / 16 9 12 5

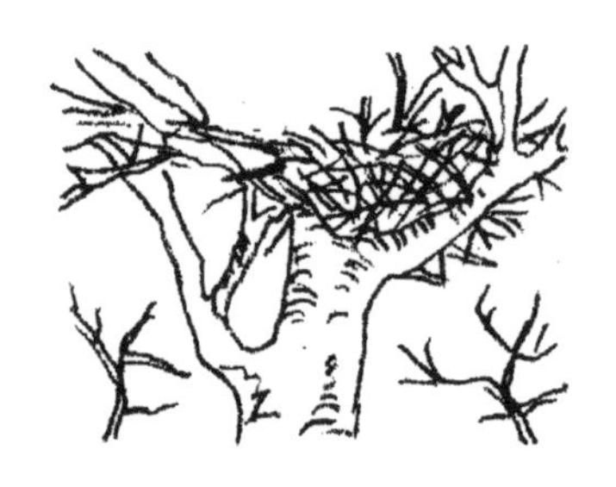

6. 5 1 7 12 5' 19 / 14 5 19 20

Answers on last page

Chipmunk: Hard to wake up. Yet wakes every 10-14 days to eat. Body temp near 32° F (0° C).

Can go without eating for months. Body temperature about 95° F (35° C) In summer it is 100° F (37° C) .

A litter mostly has 2 to 3 cubs. In Pennsylvania, where bear habitat is very good, sows occasionally have as many as 6 cubs.

Cubs born in den. Mother nurses her cubs. Body keeps them warm.

Babies born at the same time to the same mother are called a litter.

Remains aware of her surroundings. Wakens easily.

Sleeps curled up to conserve heat and keep out the cold.

Thick fur and a layer of fat.

Doesn't urinate or defecate whil sleeping. Wastes are recycled within the body.

If water leaks into a den in spring, the mother may gather material such as conifer branches. She puts them under the cubs, raising them above the water.

Newborn cubs weigh about 3/4 pound (0.34 kg) and are about the size of a gray squirrel.

In many places, black bears feast on nuts in the fall. So do chipmunks. Both animals are getting ready for winter. They sleep, or hibernate, through the winter when food is hard to find. During hibernation, the chipmunk's body temperature drops to near freezing. Its heartbeat slows down. In winter, a bear's body temperature drops by only a few degrees. Chipmunks wake up about every ten days to eat some of their stored food. Bears depend on their stored body fat. Where winters are severe, bears do without food for more than six months.

Bear cubs are born in midwinter. People used to imagine the mother bear waking in the spring to find – surprise! – she has a family to look after. But we now know that she cares for her tiny babies during the winter. Lynn Rogers, a wildlife biologist, placed a video camera inside a den. The video showed the mother nursing her cubs. She licked them dry when water from melting snow dripped on them.

Bringing Up the Cubs

L

A Bear Grows Up

Born – January or February

Weight at birth – 3/4 pound (.34 kg)

Litter size – 1 to 6; usually 2 or 3

Size at birth – 8 inches (20 cm)

Weight leaving den – 8 pounds (3.6 kg)

Weight at six months – 40 to 60 pounds (18 to 27 kg)

Age of weaning if mother is well fed – 22-30 weeks

Leave mother – 17 months

First able to give birth – 2 to 10 years, longer in areas of poor food.

Possible lifespan – 30 years

Typical lifespan in areas where bears are hunted – 4 years

C

B

D

I

K

Claw marks on trees adapted from the work of Jim Halfpenny, Ph.D. and artist Jennifer Bennett.

A father bear doesn't recognize his own cubs. In fact, he might even think they were dinner if he met them! It's up to the mother bear to teach her cubs to be safe.

The sow leaves the cubs in a **day bed** while she looks for food near by. The day bed is usually at the base of a good climbing tree. It is often covered with grass, moss, or evergreen needles. If danger is near, the cubs scramble up the tree.

When cubs climb, they hug the tree trunk and bound up with their hind feet in unison. Their claws leave an arc of five puncture marks in the bark. When a bear slides down, it leaves long scratch patterns.

Cubs nurse until they are about six months old, but even before they are weaned the sow is teaching them to find food. The cubs learn to tear open logs in search of insect larvae. They look for young shoots. Early spring is a tough time – there's not much food for a hungry bear. Depending on where the bears live, the mother might find a hidden elk calf or deer fawn to eat.

Bear cubs love to play. Playing is an important way for them to learn how to act towards other bears. They learn how to be **dominant**, the boss. They also find out how to be **subordinate**, the follower. After a long playtime on a hot day, bears cool off by lying in the water, panting, or resting in the shade with their undersides against the ground.

Study the picture and decide where you might find the following:

_____ Cub nursing

_____ Cubs playing

_____ Good location for a day bed

_____ A tree where a cub climbed up

_____ A tree where a cub climbed down

_____ Where would a bear cool off?

_____ A place to find grubs

_____ Approaching danger

_____ A place to escape a male bear or hungry wolf

_____ Possible food

How do bears say hello?

Have you noticed that humans have different ways of communicating with each other? Often we use our voices. Other times we might just use our face or hands to get a message across. Bears also communicate in several ways.

Bears use three different languages.

1. Sound — grunts, squeals, moans, puffing and many other sounds
2. Special scents — markings
3. Body language — body positions and movements

What are these bears saying? Look closely at the face, ears and body. **Match each bear to a message.** Messages can be used more than once.

Messages

Hello!
Move back
I'm curious
I feel threatened
I smell something
I am nervous

Answers on last page

A Bear's Neighborhood

Bears are always on the move in search of food. Cubs follow their mother, learning the ways of bears. Other bears travel alone. Each bear usually stays in its own area or **home range**. A female marks her range with urine. She leaves claw marks on trees. This lets other bears know that the area is taken. Bears usually respect one another's range. The trespasser is mostly just chased off. But fights can break out.

Bite mark on a telephone pole (4 inches or about 10 centimeters across)

Some trees are **bulletin board** trees. Bears leave a message on the tree by rubbing their backs against the trunk. The scent or a tuft of hair caught in the rough bark announces that the bear was in the area. The bear may turn its head backwards, leaving a **bite mark** on the tree.

The amount of space a bear needs depends on the landscape, the density of bears, and the quality of the food supply. The male's range is larger than the female's. In northern Wisconsin, the average range for a male is 36 square miles and 7 square miles for a female.

If a quarter equals 7 square miles, how many home ranges can you fit into this landscape? A range needs water, shrubs for food, and a least one big tree. ____________

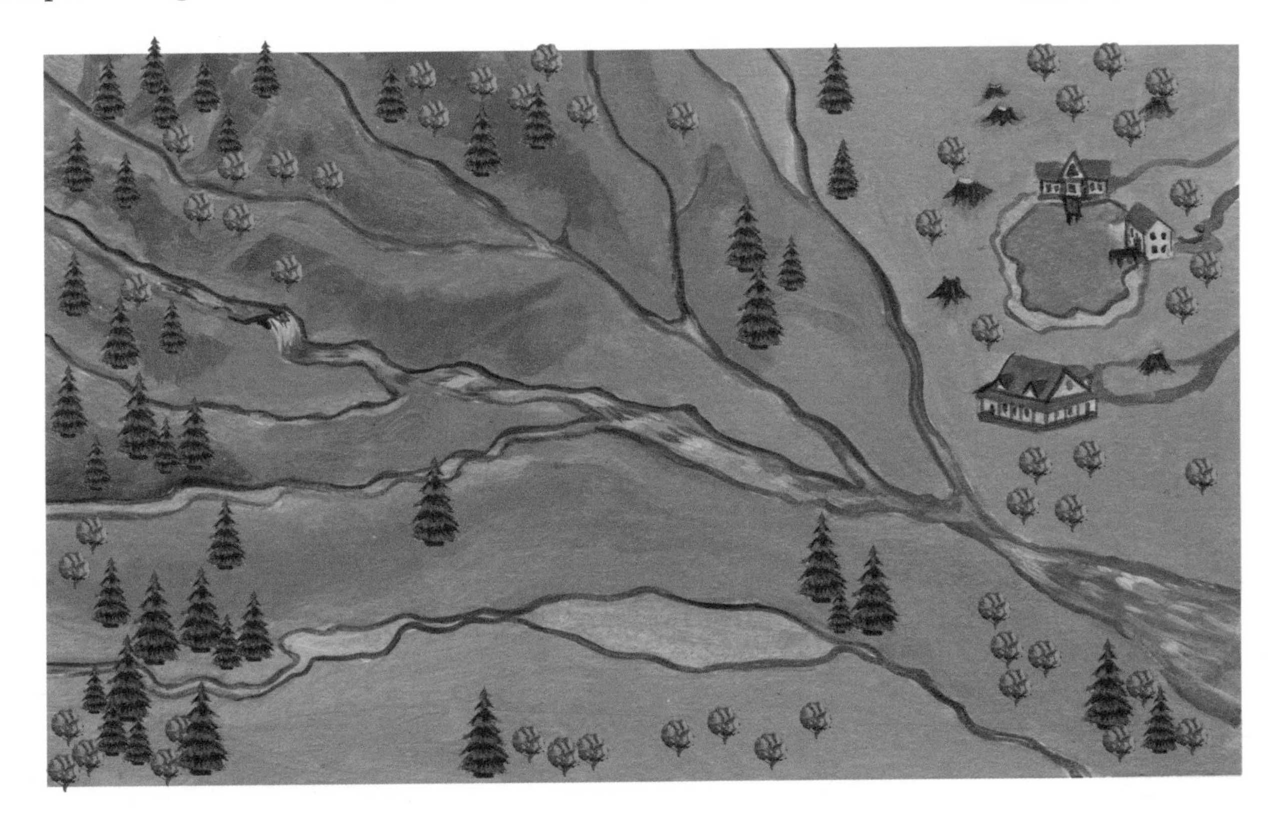

When the cubs are about 17 months old, their mother is ready to mate and start a new family. This means that the cubs have to find a new home. Female cubs usually set up their ranges within their mother's territory. Young males usually have to look farther afield. They may travel as far as 100 miles in search of open space. Starting life on his own is hard for the young male.

Answers on last page

At Home in a Southern Swamp

An animal's **habitat** provides **food**, **water**, **shelter** and **space** arranged in such a way that the animal can live. Black bears are found in many different types of habitat. They are usually found in forests. But some live in the Labrador in the far north where there are no trees. Some live in southern swamps.

In states like Florida, Georgia, and Louisiana, food is available all year round. Bears in these states do not need to hibernate. The Florida black bear has a period called winter denning, lasting from late December to early May. During this time pregnant females go without food and give birth to their cubs. Males and non-pregnant females also find dens. However, they often leave their den to feed and find another one.

If a bear from the north is given a winter vacation in the South, he sleeps the time away just as he did back home.

The letters mark important elements of a bear's habitat. Identify which one (or ones) each letter represents.

A. __________ **B.** __________ **C.** __________ **D.** __________ **E.** __________
F. __________ **G.** __________ **H.** __________ **I.** __________

I
G
H
F
E

What is for dinner?

Bears are big animals whose food comes in small packages. What black bears eat depends on the season and where the live. They eat ants and grubs, berries and nuts, leaves, and roots. They also eat carrion (dead meat) and, in some places, fish. They can kill small deer fawns or elk calves, but in spite of their size, their long claws, and their strong teeth, they are not fierce predators. Plants make up most of their diet. They will generally pass up meat if better food is available.

Bears are **omnivores**. They feed on both plants and animals. Humans are omnivores, too. Bears like the food we eat – even the food we throw away as garbage. This can lead to problems – for us and for the bear.

Bears are not tidy eaters. They can pluck a single berry from a bush with their flexible lips and long tongues. But they may also snap off an oak branch as big around as your arm to get at the acorns. They use their claws to pull apart a stump or a log in search of grubs. Their untidy ways help logs and rotting wood to decompose (break down) quickly. This is part of the cycle of returning nutrients to the soil

Bears help spread seeds. Pits of fruits, such as the wild plum, may be carried a long way before they pass out in the bear's **scat**, or droppings. The seeds then grow in another place.

Unscrambled the clues to find food on a bear's menu. Write the names on the lines below.

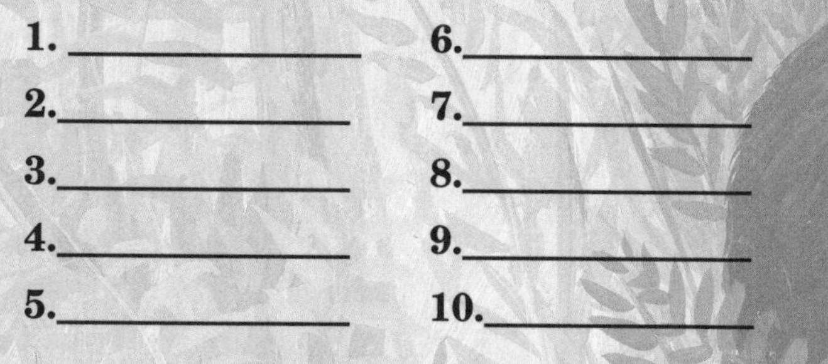

1. ______________ **6.** ______________

2. ______________ **7.** ______________

3. ______________ **8.** ______________

4. ______________ **9.** ______________

5. ______________ **10.** ______________

In real life, plants on these pages are not all found together.

Answers on last page

1. CALBK HCREIRSE

2. VCIEESRIRESBER

3. NOEYH

4. LEUB EERBRIS

5. NARICOR

10. PSPELA

6. HERCKERBULISE

7. MLSAL SMMMLSA

8. NSORCA

9. HEECB USTN

Bear Math

A male bear is born in February and weighs a little less than 1 pound. He nurses and grows rapidly. In spring when he leaves the den, he has gained 9 pounds. He now weighs ________(A) pounds. He drinks rich milk and also learns to find his own food. By late fall he weighs eight times as much as he did when he left the den in the spring. When he starts hibernating, he weighs ________ (B) pounds. During the winter he loses 20 pounds. He now weighs ________ (C) pounds. In the spring, his mother is ready to start another family and chases him away. Over summer and fall he grows fat on a diet of grubs, berries, and acorns. He gains 90 pounds. By his second winter, he weighs ________ (D) pounds.

He continues to grow, losing weight in the winter and gaining more in the summer when food is abundant until he reaches full growth at about 12 years. He could weigh anywhere from 125 to 600 pounds. Most male black bears weigh 250 pounds. Once a great big one was caught that weighed 880 pounds.

Answers on last page

How would the sizes of the bear be different for a female bear? What happens to a female's weight when she is nursing cubs? What would happen if it was a bad year for bear food?

Spring Menu

Sweet Inner Bark (Cambium)

New Flowers

New Leaves

Grasses

Skunk Cabbage

Ant Pupae

Horsetails

Salmonberry

Summer Menu

Serviceberries

Cow Parsnip

Wild Strawberries

Ants

A Bear's Life

A bear's life isn't easy. Bears need food, water and shelter. They need good health, good social skills and good luck. Some die from accidents or starvation. Some are killed by hunters or poachers.

Can you survive as a bear? Can you find enough food to get you through the winter? Can you live long enough to have cubs? Find out by playing the game on the following pages.

You will need:

- Four objects (paper or pebbles) numbered 1, 2, 3, and 4. Place them in a container, such as a paper bag or hat. If you use dice, roll again if you get 5 or 6.
- Pencil and paper to keep track of your score.
- A playing piece for each player. You can use a bear sticker on a firm backing, or a pebble or coin, or trace one of the bears, cut it out, color it, and tape it to a penny.
- At least three den tokens for each player. They could be pebbles, twigs or coins.
- You also need the game board on the next page.

Directions:

1. One or more people can play. More than one bear can win.
2. Your goal is to survive and have cubs. You need to collect at least 3 den tokens and 175 points. (A female bear needs to be 3 years old and weigh about 175 pounds before she becomes a mother.)
3. Place your playing piece on START. Decide who goes first.
4. Draw a number and move your playing piece. Follow instructions and keep track of your score at each move.
5. Watch for places where you have to stop and wait until next turn to move on.
6. Watch for squares with arrows telling you to take a different path.
7. If you land on the RELOCATION site, you are captured and sent to the WILDERNESS. If you land on the RELOCATION three times, you are shot. (You can start again as a new bear).
8. Each time you spend the winter in a den collect a DEN TOKEN. You will lose points in the winter den because you are not eating and lose weight.
9. If you lose all your points, you starve. You can start over as a new bear.
10. When you have three tokens and weigh at least 155 pounds, you can take the path to the final den. You don't need an exact number to finish.

START
At birth you weigh about half a pound.

Get fat on mother's milk. 20 points

Take a nap.

Drink mother's milk. 20 points

Beat other cubs to nursing. 20 points

Next turn adventure out of the den.

Leave the den.

Learn which plants are good to eat. 30 points

Practice climbing trees. 30 points

Turn over log to find bugs. 30 points

Nurse in a sheltered spot. 20 points

Find bees' nest in tree. 20 points

Take a campground detour. Raid bird feeder. You are a problem bear. Lose 20 points

Pose for a picture.

Find food by tipping garbage can. 20 points

Rob some dog food. 10 points

Infested with ticks. Lose 20 points

Snap up insects. 10 points

House built in your feeding grounds. Lose 20 points

Steal camper's backpack for food. 10 points

Steal food from a car. 20 points

Relocation
Scientists move you to WILDERNESS. If you land here 3 times you are killed as a nuisance bear.

Feast on blueberries. 20 points

Killed by poachers who are after gall bladder and bear paws for illegal market.

Find your way back to a campground.

WILDERNESS Relocation Site. Even numbers go left, odd numbers go right.

Eat nuts. 20 points

Fall out of tree. Lose 10 points

Stop to nurse. 20 points

Sleep in den one turn.

STOP — Winter sleep with mother. Lose 30 points. Take a den token.

Stop to nurse. 20 points

Feast on blueberries. 30 points

Learn to find nuts. 40 points

Sniff out ants' nest. 30 points

Climb to tree top to avoid being killed by adult male bear.

Struck by vehicle. Lose turn recovering.

Eat acorns or other nuts. 40 points

Hit by boulder rolling down hill. Lose 10 points recovering.

If you have 1 or 2 den tokens and fewer than 155 points go left or if you have 3 tokens and over 155 points you meet your mate and take this trail.

→155

Step on this scale.

Your weight is equal to your points

Stop at Weigh Station

Find a few nuts on ground to build fat reserves for winter. 10 points

Rake leaves toward den to use for bedding material.

Sleep in den one turn.

STOP — Winter sleep Lose 30 points. Take a den token.

While in den, radio collared by scientists, or collar replaced.

Food scarce. Lose 20 points

Find seeds buried by squirrels. 20 points

Climb tree to eat spring buds. 20 points

Eat sweet inner bark from trees. 20 points

Feast on clover. 20 points

Broken teeth. Take detour.

Sick from poisonous berries. Lose 10 points.

Sick with intestinal worms Lose 10 points.

Black flies keep bothering your face and eyes. Lose 10 points

Starving. Lose 30 points looking for food.

Eat spring flowers and leaves. 20 points

Dine on grasses. 40 points

Pluck individual berries from a branch. 40 points

Dig around tree roots to find food. 20 points

Stand on hind feet and sniff for food. 10 points

Miserable with mange, a skin disease. Lose 20 points.

Break leg in fall. Lose 10 points recovering.

Stuff full of berries and other fruits. 20 points .

Fatten up on acorns and nuts. 20 points

Find apples. 20 points

Climb trees to find more nuts. 20 points

FINISH Prepare den, have babies, take a long winter sleep.

Hide and Seek

The bears that lived near the Elwha River in the Olympic National Park had not tasted salmon for 90 years. Engineers were planning to take out two dams so that salmon could come back up the river to spawn. Wildlife biologist, Kim Sager, wondered how this would change the behavior of the bears. Would it affect their seasonal routes through the forest? First, she needed to find out where the bears were spending their time now.

Tracking bears in the deep forest was like a game of hide-and-seek, where Kim was always the seeker. But she had high-tech instruments to help her. First,

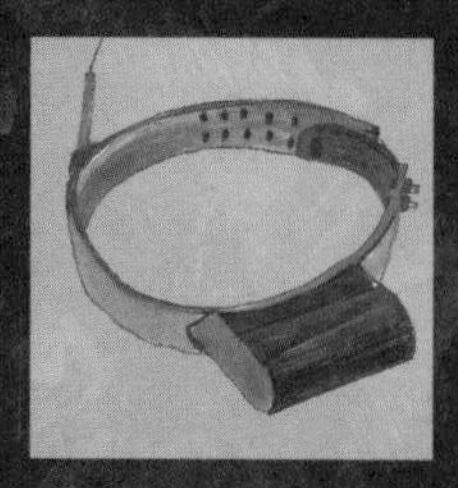

Kim and her co-worker Dave Manson trapped bears in foot snares with road-killed deer for bait. They then fastened radio collars around the bears' necks. Each collar sent out a different beeping signal, so they could tell which bear they were tracking. The signals were picked up on a receiver with an antenna. The signal was strongest when the antenna pointed directly at the bear. With the help of a compass, Kim and Dave located the bear. They marked the location in their notebooks and on a map.

Some bears were fitted with Global Positioning System (GPS) collars. Satellites help locate the collared bear on the ground. Kim and Dave flew over each bear about every two months. They downloaded the bear's location data into a hand-held command unit. GPS collars provide more information than radio collars, but they cost a lot more. An Argos collar sends data directly to a computer. It costs even more.

Help Kim and Dave find two bears. They are holding their antennae so that they point to the strongest signal from one of the bear. Draw a line from each antenna and you will find the bear. Kim and Dave track a second bear and check its location using compasses. Kim's compass reads 60˚ and Dave's reads 320˚. Draw a line from each compass. Again, the second bear is where the lines meet. Finding the bear from two or more spots is called triangulation.

In the Field - Bear Watchers

To learn about bear behavior, researchers need to study bears in the wild. They do **field research**. Before starting, they decide on the question they want to answer. They might want to find out how a bear can live for six months without eating or drinking. Or how bears communicate with one another. Or what is a bear's favorite food. The next step is to come up with a good guess at the answer. This is called a **hypothesis**. The investigators then make field observations, design experiments, or read articles in science journals to discover what other researchers have found. Most scientists do all three.

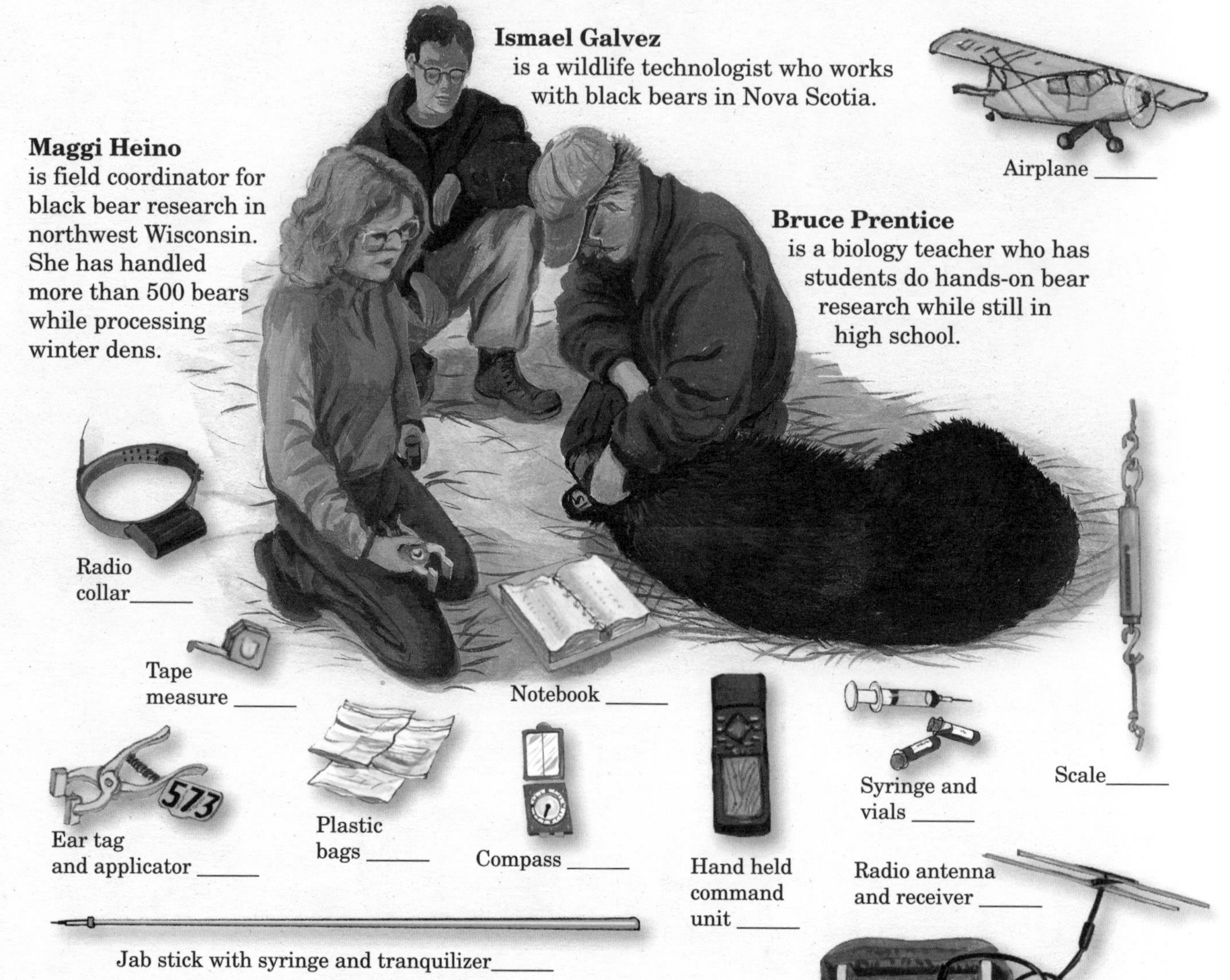

Scientists use many different types of equipment to study bears.
Can you match each type with its job?

A. Shows direction, helps scientist locate bear.
B. Shows bear's location by sending radio signals from small transmitter.
C. Picks up signal from radio collar. Helps scientist locate bear.
D. Puts bear into a deep sleep from a safe distance. (Sedates bear).
E. Weighs bear.
F. Draws blood sample for health tests.
G. Measures size of bear.
H. Container for hair, scat and other samples
I. Placed on bear for future identification.
J. Place to record information.
K. Used to find location from air.
L. Receives data from a GPS collar.

Answers on last page

In the Lab - Bear Detectives

After gathering information in the field, scientists continue to learn about bears in their offices and labs. They may use computers to analyze their data. They may use microscopes to get a closer look at their finds.

Sue Mansfield learns a lot about bears without actually seeing them. She is a **scat** detective. (Scat is what scientists call animal droppings.) By examining scat, Sue can tell how long ago the animal passed through the area. She can guess at its size. The appearance of the scat may provide a clue to its diet. Sue can tell if a bear fed on strawberries or blueberries or grass. If hair is present, it's usually the bear's own hair from grooming. Occasionally hair from a small mammal or carrion shows up.

Sue usually finds a lot of plant material. This is because bears eat lots of plants. But it is also because plant material is harder to digest than animal material. More of it ends up in the scat.

One day in late September, a mother bear named June and her two cubs disappeared from the study area. June's signal was found 15 miles away in a remote roadless area.

When the bears returned, Sue became a detective. She found trace bits of acorn in June's scat. On the day June left, the wind was from the Boundary Waters area to the NE, where oak trees grew. June had likely smelled acorns in the wind. She and her cubs had gone looking for one more tasty treat before it was time for their long winter sleep.

Take a wild guess! How many raspberry seeds were in a pile of bear scat on Sue's desk?

100 1500 3000

How many hazelnuts did a black bear eat in one day?

56 809 2605

Hairy Clues

Like detectives in a crime lab, biologists can use DNA evidence to follow the wanderings of bears in the forest. The scientist sets up barbed wire traps in places where bears often travel. When a bear rubs against the wire, it leaves a few hairs behind. The scientist extracts the DNA from the hairs. The pattern of the DNA is unique for each bear, but related bears have similar DNA. The scientist can tell if hairs are from a mother and her cubs or from unrelated bears.

How is a bear's tooth like a tree stump?

You can tell a bear's age by looking at a cross section of its tooth. It's like counting rings on a tree stump. In good food years, the spaces between the lines in the tooth are wider than in bad years. The space is narrower in years when a sow has cubs. The dark lines are laid down in winter. It takes a lot of food energy to produce milk. How old was this bear?

A Man who Walks with Bears

Lynn Rogers' goal is to discover ways for people and bears to co-exist. He wants to keep bears safe. Problems arise when a bear becomes a nuisance while trying to get food. Lynn knows many of the bears that live in the woods around his Wildlife Research Institute in northern Minnesota. After years of studying their behavior he has gained their trust. He knows when he can be near them and when they want more space. Some bears are so at ease with Lynn that he can put a radio collar on a mother with cubs without using a tranquilizer.

Radio collars help Lynn keep track of his study bears as they make their living in the forest. He learns even more by walking alongside a bear as it visits its secret places. A young female he named Whiteheart became so comfortable around Lynn that when he followed her through the forest she seemed to forget he was there. While she napped next to a favorite old white pine, Lynn rested nearby. He noted everything she ate — three dandelions, a tongueful of berries, two snips of grass, a mouthful of ants. Eating was her main occupation. Meantime, Lynn went hungry. Even on a walk that lasted all day and all night, he went without food. The smell of human food would have distracted Whiteheart.

Over the years, Lynn has learned bear talk. When a mother wants to be with her cubs or wants them to come down from a tree and follow, she might make a grunting sound. A moaning sound means she's afraid. So does teeth-clacking. Bears blow and sometimes slap a tree when they are nervous or feel crowded. Cubs make a motor-like sound when they a nursing.

From this list of sounds, choose the sound that might fit the bear's situation: Blowing, screaming, moaning, yawning, teeth-clacking, motor-like noise, grunting, slapping tree or ground

Mother is concerned about cubs ________

Fear ______________________

Nervous ______________________

Terrified cub ______________________

Resting bear feeling a little tension

____

Pleasure sound while nursing

____

To hear real bear sounds, visit the North American Bear Center at www.bear.org

Bluff Charge

A scared bear sometimes charges, but it's just bluffing! It blows and slams its feet down hard as it bounds forward looking very ferocious. It stops several yards—or even just a few feet—short of the threat and then turns and runs away. Lynn has had bears do this toward him many times and never make contact.

Answers on last page

Black Bears All Over

Some animals, like polar bears, need a special type of habitat, but black bears can live in many different habitats. They occur in most states, across Canada, and into Mexico. In northern Canada, they become rare toward the tree line (where trees do not grow because of the severe climate). They are absent north of the tree line, except in Labrador. The map is marked with symbols that tell the status of bears in different areas. **Color the areas where bears are numerous (N) blue. Color areas where bears are few (F) yellow and absent (A) red.**

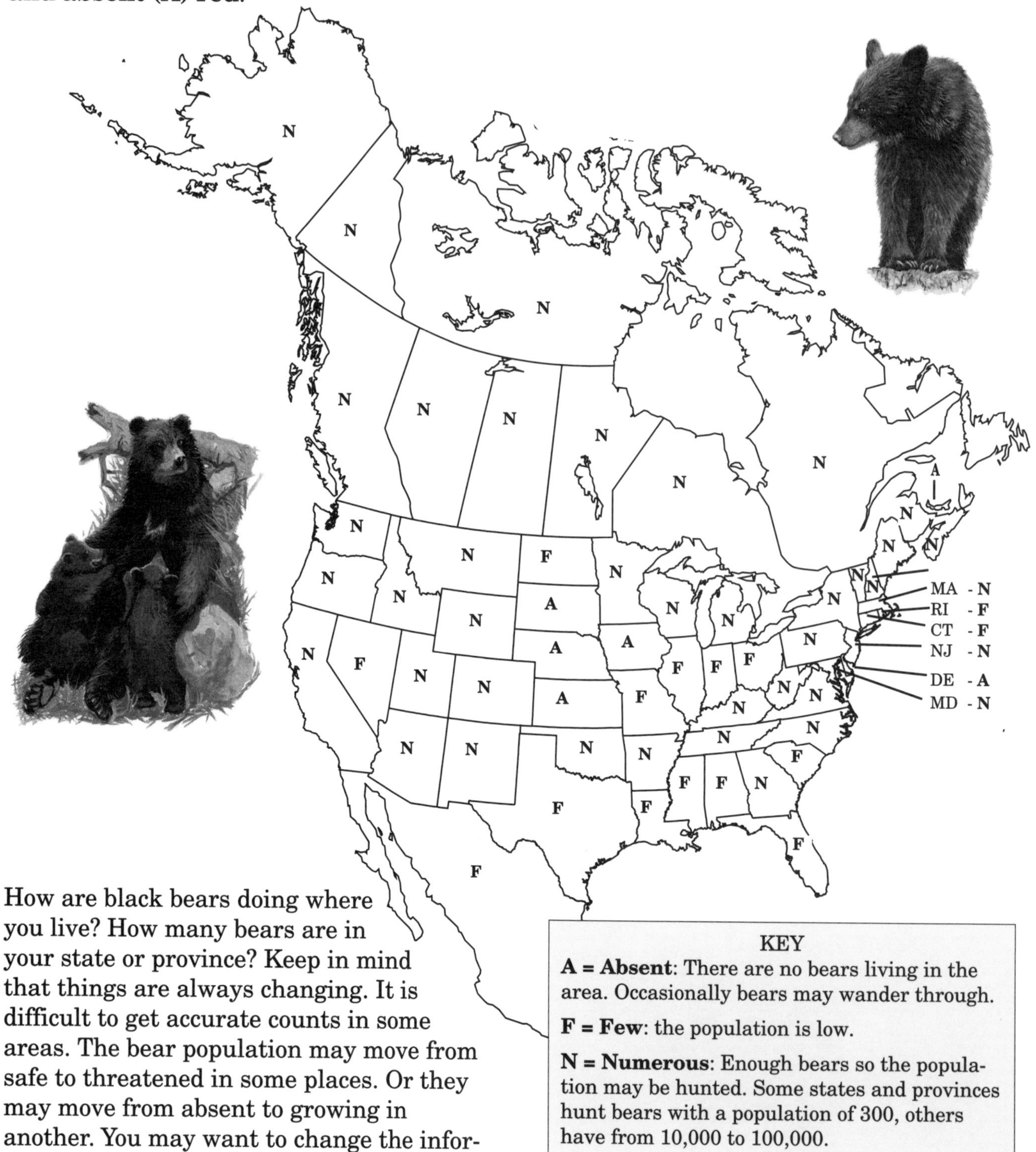

How are black bears doing where you live? How many bears are in your state or province? Keep in mind that things are always changing. It is difficult to get accurate counts in some areas. The bear population may move from safe to threatened in some places. Or they may move from absent to growing in another. You may want to change the information on this map if you find new facts.

KEY

A = Absent: There are no bears living in the area. Occasionally bears may wander through.

F = Few: the population is low.

N = Numerous: Enough bears so the population may be hunted. Some states and provinces hunt bears with a population of 300, others have from 10,000 to 100,000.

Headline News

A black bear can live for up to 30 years, but most wild bears don't live beyond 3 to 5 years. The black bear's deadliest enemy has no fur, no fangs, no claws and a poor sense of smell. Most bears are killed by hunters or poachers. A few are killed by vehicles. Cubs may die from starvation or by falling from trees. Sometimes they are attacked by predators.

A wildlife biologist's aim is to keep the bear population healthy. Tracking the number of bears in an area helps decide the length of the hunting season and how many hunters should take part. Responsible hunters obey the laws and provide information that aids researchers.

Poaching is illegal hunting. Poachers kill bears at any time of the year, even in areas where bears are endangered. They often take only a few parts and leave most of the animal. The gall bladder is a small organ that helps a bear digest its food. Some people believe that dried bear gall is a powerful medicine. The paws are used to make bear paw soup.

Look at the headlines below and decide if the article is about hunting, poaching, or an accident. Circle hunting headlines green, poaching headlines red, and accidents orange.

1 **Dead bear found near busy highway**

2 **Hibernating bear killed in den.**

3 Two dead cubs in garbage can.
Gall bladders missing.

4 Bag limits: One license per year; at least 100 pounds live weight.
Females with cubs may not be taken.

5 *Hunters asked to spare bears with radio collars.*

6 **Loose rock sends cub to its death.**
Falls into Yellowstone River.

7 Bear dies
after eating coyote poisoned by rancher.

8 **Bear paw soup tops $1000 overseas.**

9 Spring bear season April 1-
Send in premolar tooth to determine

Visiting Bear Country

The sign said BEAR COUNTRY. "Black bears like to pull people out of their tents for a midnight snack," Reed told his sister.

"Not true!" Kendall answered. "Scientists follow them through the forest in complete safety."

Who was right?

By speaking loudly, Reed and Kendall were following a basic rule for traveling in bear country. Make lots of noise so that you don't surprise a bear.

Look at the picture. What have people done right? What have they done wrong? (See answer page)

Bear Country - Stay Safe!

- Travel with a group.
- Keep dogs on a leash.
- If you do see a bear, keep your distance.
- Never use food to lure a bear closer for photos.
- Don't camp where there are signs of bear.
- Cook away from tent.
- Don't keep food in tent.
- Put food and garbage in sealed containers. Hang packs between trees at least 10 feet up, 6 feet from any branches and 100 yards from the tent.
- Don't keep cosmetics and ChapStick® in tent.
- Don't sleep in same clothes used for cooking.
- Use flashlight at night.
- Keep campsite clean and pack out garbage.
- Secure food and cosmetics in a vehicle if possible.

TO BACK COUNTRY
BEAR BIN
SUN SCREEN

Unwelcome Guests

Seeing a mother bear and her cubs eating berries near a campground can be exciting. A bear with its nose in the garbage can next to the house is a less welcome sight. We don't appreciate bears that rip bird feeders apart and knock over beehives. More people are building homes in forested areas. This leads to more conflicts with bears, especially in years when natural food is scarce.

Match the bear fact to a possible consequence:

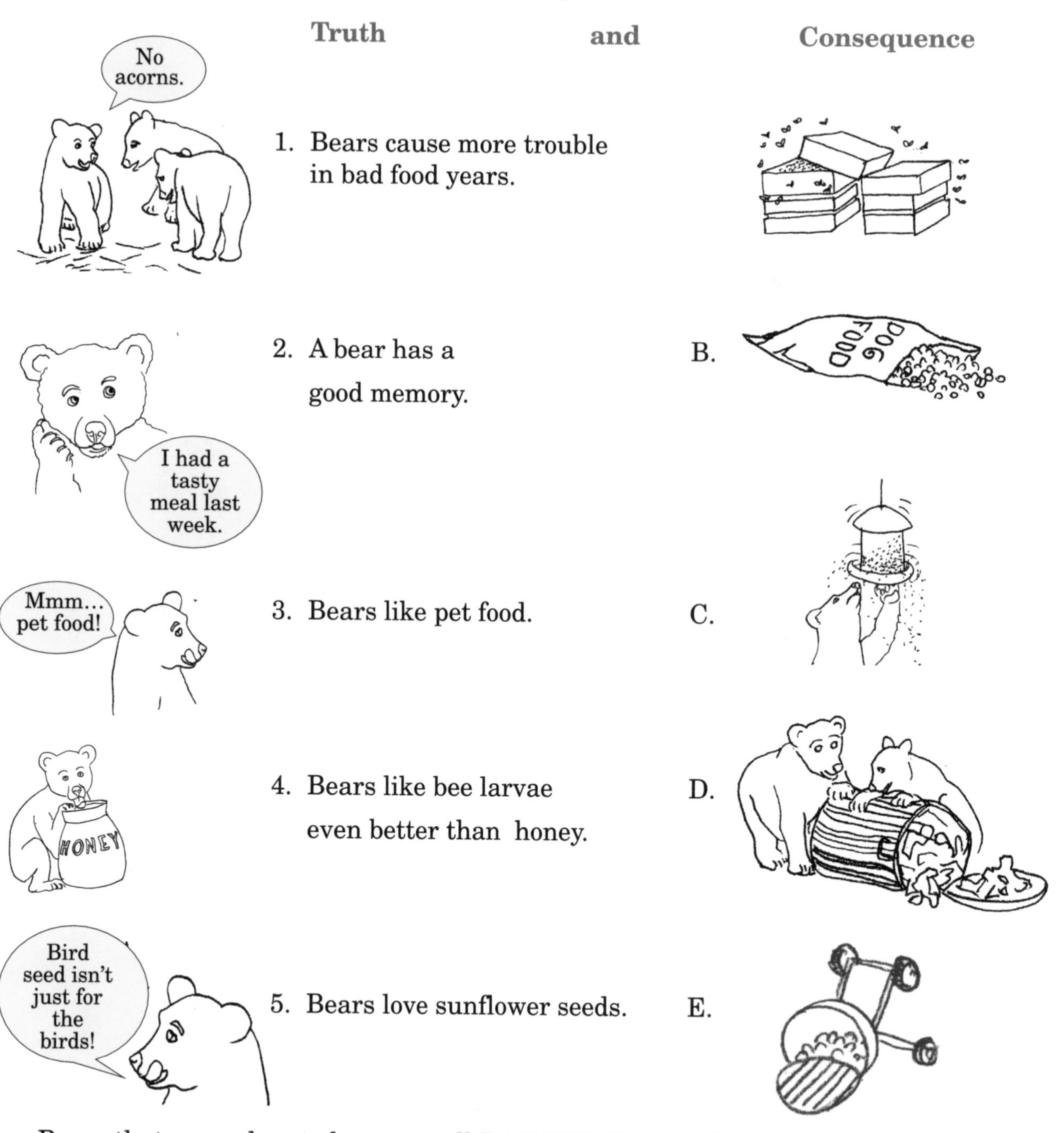

Truth and Consequence

1. Bears cause more trouble in bad food years.
2. A bear has a good memory. B.
3. Bears like pet food. C.
4. Bears like bee larvae even better than honey. D.
5. Bears love sunflower seeds. E.

Bears that come close to houses spell DANGER. But the danger is mostly to the bear. Such bears are labeled "nuisance bears." A nuisance bear may be captured, tagged and released in another area. If it returns - and it often does - the bear is usually shot. Some bears are not given a second chance.

Answers on last page

Bears are strong, intelligent animals with a good memory for food sources. Their sense of smell is seven times better than that of a bloodhound. People who live in bear country should take steps to avoid attracting bears. What are some things we can do?

There are many different kinds of bear-proof garbage containers, from simple family cans to large trash lockers for groups of people.

When a forest is criss-crossed by roads and broken into small areas by patches of cleared land, it is said to be **fragmented**. It's hard for bears to live in a fragmented forest without trespassing on somebody's property. Where home ranges no longer overlap, finding a mate can be a problem. With the big trees gone, cubs can't climb to safety.

In a fragmented forest, bears have to travel farther in their search for food. Many black bears are killed crossing highways. In some places, people have installed bear-friendly underpasses or bridges lined with shrubs and bushes to help bears cross busy roads safely. These crossings help other wildlife, too.

Bears in the Sky

The ancient Greeks saw pictures in the night sky. We call the groups of stars that form these pictures constellations. One of these pictures is **Ursa Major**, the Great Bear. Ursa Major includes the **Big Dipper**, a group of stars that is easy to recognize. The handle of the Big Dipper forms the bear's tail and the cup is its flank. The bear seems to keep changing its position. It sometimes stands on its feet, sometimes lies on its back and sometimes rises up on its hind legs, ready to fight.

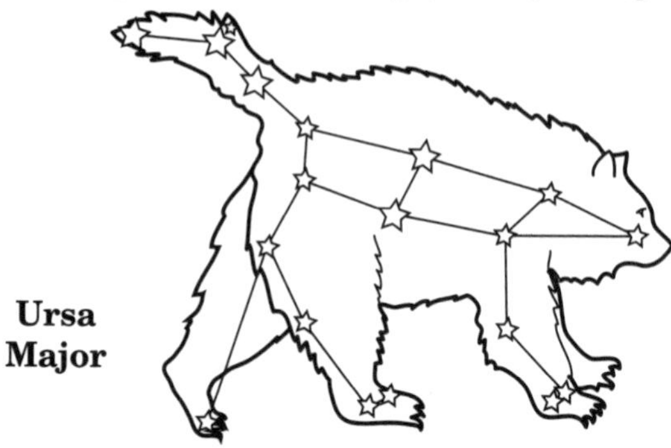

Ursa Major

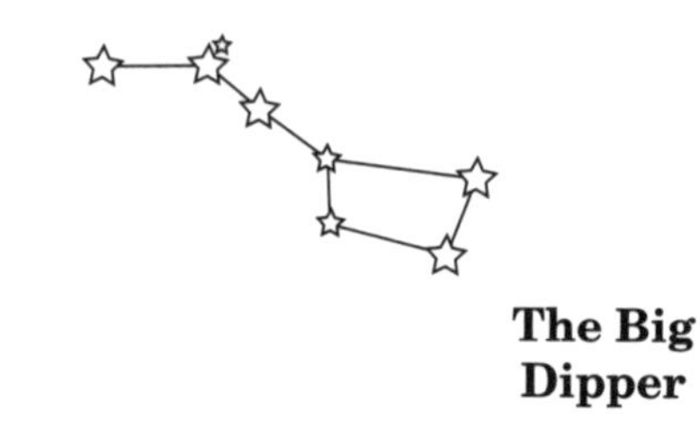

The Big Dipper

In other cultures, people see the Big Dipper as a cart or wagon, or a plow. The Native Americans, like the Greeks, saw a bear. But their bear is made up of fewer stars than the Greek constellation – only the four stars that form the bowl of the dipper. The three bright stars along the handle are hunters following the bear. The little star close to the middle hunter is his dog. Another constellation that we call the Northern Crown is the bear's den.

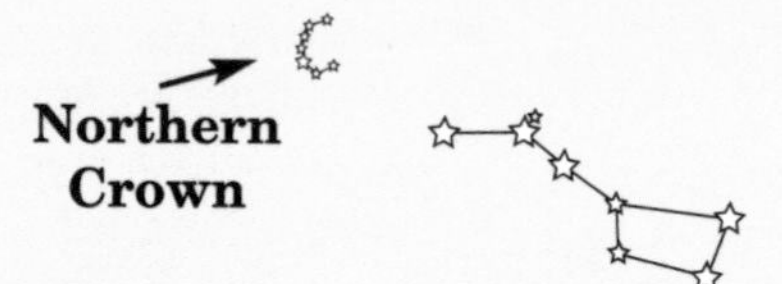

The legend of the bear begins in the spring when she emerges from her den. The hunters are hungry after the long winter. The hunt is on! All spring, they chase the bear across the night sky.

During the summer, night after night, they follow the bear's tracks. It is almost fall when the catch up with her. She stands on her hind legs, ready to defend herself.

In the fall, when the constellation is low in the sky, the hunters finally close in and kill the bear. As they carve up the flesh, the bear's blood drips onto the leaves of the sumac and maple, turning them bright red.

During the winter, the bear's skeleton is still visible in the night sky. But that is not the end of the story. The bear's spirit enters a newborn baby bear in the nearby den. In the spring, when the bear emerges from her den, the hunt begins all over again.

Bears in the Forest

Bears are an important part of Native American history. The bear hunt was treated with great ceremony and respect. Bear meat provided rich food. The sweet fat was used as oil for frying and as a base for medicines. Bearskins were prized as robes and for trading. Some clans, or family groups, had bears as symbols or totems. Many Native American stories and songs that feature bears give them human-like qualities.

Cherokee bear hunters still sing the songs that the Ani Tsaguhi (Ah-nee Jah-goo-hee) clansmen taught them. The hunters learned the songs on the day that a young boy named Yonva led his clan out of the valley.

Earlier in the summer, Yonva was gone each day from sunrise till sunset. Although his parents begged and scolded, the boy would not stay home. Then they noticed that he was growing long brown hair all over his body. All their son would say was that life was better in the woods on the mountain than down in the valley. "There I eat well without working," he explained.

When the rest of the clan heard about the easy life in the woods, they begged to go there too.

"First you must fast for seven days," Yonva told them.

So they all fasted. On the seventh evening the boy showed them the way to the mountains.

When the other clans in the valley heard that the Ani Tsaguhi were leaving, they sent their hunters to ask them to stay. But the Ani Tsaguhi would not listen. "We are on our way to a place where we shall eat well and not have to work so hard," they said.

Then Yonva added, "When you are hungry, you may come into our woods. If you sing the songs we teach you, we will give you our flesh. Do not be afraid to kill us for we are the bear people and we shall be here always."

While the hunters were learning the songs, they noticed that the Ani Tsaguhi had grown long brown hair all over their bodies. And when the Ani Tsaguhi headed off into the woods, the hunters saw no people – only a group of bears.

Famous Bear Tales

Bears are popular characters in stories. Pair up the start and ending of each story. Write its name under the picture that goes with it. Answers on last page

The Haunted Forest

Fiona and Gillian were staying at their Grandpa's cabin in the woods. Grandpa was dozing by the fire and the girls were looking out of the window. The moon cast a silvery light on the meadow. Beyond the meadow was the dark forest. Suddenly a white shape appeared out of the trees.

"What's that?" Gillian asked in a quivery voice.

"It's a ghost!" Fiona answered. "Grandpa! There's a ghost out there! A ghost with two black shadows!"

By the time Grandpa came over to the window, the ghost was gone. All he could see was the silvery meadow surrounded by dark trees.

"We're snug and safe here in the cabin," Grandpa told the girls. "Tomorrow we'll go on a ghost hunt and you may be surprised at what we find."

The next morning, the meadow looked quite different in the sunshine. The girls led Grandpa across the meadow to the place where they'd seen the ghost. "Look here … and … and over here … and here!" Grandpa said.

Can you find the clues in the picture below that helped Grandpa and the girls solve the ghost mystery? Turn the page and see if you are right.

*Did you find the bear footprints near a huckleberry bush? The bear stripped the leaves from its branches. She left a tuft of **white** hair in the rough bark when she rubbed her back against the tree. Did you spot cub claw marks on a tree trunk and the pile of scat at the base of the big tree?*

"You are lucky girls!" Grandpa told Fiona and Gillian. "What you saw was a *white* bear. The two dark shadows were her cubs."

"Can a white bear have black cubs?" Fiona asked.

"Yes, indeed!" Grandpa answered. "But you weren't so very far off when you said you'd seen a ghost! The white bear — or kermode bear — is called the **spirit bear** by some Native Americans. They believe it has special powers."

Tracking Bear Words

Solve the crossword puzzle. You'll have made your own glossary and index.

Across

4. One of the three kinds of bears found in North America (p. 4)
5. You can tell bear's age from its cross section (p. 25)
8. May spell death for bears (p. 33)
9. Mother bear leaves her cubs in a _____ bed while she hunts (p. 11)
11. Bear droppings (p. 25)
12. Teeth for tearing wood apart (p. 6)
14. Male bear (p. 8)
16. Dead meat (p. 9)
18. Winter sleep (p. 9)
19. Where a cub may find safety (p. 11)
20. Favorite fall food (p. 17)
21. White phase of black bear (p. 38)
23. Cubs born at the same time to a sow (p. 9)

Down

1. A female bear (p. 8)
2. Has a shoulder hump and dished-in face (p. 5)
3. Illegal hunters (p. 29)
6. Favorite late summer food (p. 18)
7. What bears may raid for food (p. 33)
9. Where bears sleep in winter (p. 8)
10. Worn around neck and sends signals. _________ collar (p. 22)
12. Young bear (p. 9)
13. Where a bear finds shelter, space, food and water (p. 14)
15. Feeds on plants and animals (p. 16)
17. Bears tear up logs looking for these (p. 33)
22. Worn on ear for identification (p. 24)

Answers on last page

Answers

p. 5 1 – Black; 2 – Black; 3 – Grizzly; 4 – Black; 5 – Can't tell; 6 – Can't tell

p. 6 1 – Cheek Teeth; 2 – Canines; 3 – Diastema; 4 – Incisors

p. 7 1 – Tongue; 2 – Eyes and Nose; 3 – Canine teeth and Claws; 4 – Diastema; 5 – Nose; 6 – Cheek teeth and Stomach; 7 – Claws; 8 – Lips and tongue; 9 – Ears (nose only works in one direction).

p. 8 1 – Hollow in tree; 2 – Cave; 3 – Crawl Space (under house or shed); 4 – Culvert; 5 – In brush pile; 6 – Eagle's nest (Found in northern Wisconsin in 2004 — an unusual place for a den!). Bears are also be found under logs, among boulders, and even on top of the ground.

p. 11 Nursing - I; Playing - H; Location for day bed - A,K; Up - C; Down - B; Cool off - E. F; Find grubs - G; Approaching danger - D; Place to escape - A, L, B, C ; Food sources J, G, I.

p. 12 A. Hello; B. I feel threatened; C. I'm curious; D. I smell something; E. Hello; F. I am nervous, G. Move Back

p. 13 About 15 females. Males overlap with females. There would be room for 2 to 3 males overlapping with females in this area.

p. 14-15 A– Space; B– Food (armadillo); C– Food (alligator eggs); D– Food (berries); E– Food (berries); F– Water; G– Shelter and Space; H– Shelter; H– Shelter and Space.

p. 16-17 1 – Black cherries; 2 – Serviceberries; 3 – Honey in bees' nest; 4 – Blueberries; 5 – Carrion (such as dead deer); 6 – Huckleberries; 7 – Small mammals (very small part of their diet; 8 – Acorns; 9 – Beech nuts; 10 – Apples.

p. 18 A – 10; B – 80; C – 60; D – 150.

p. 24 A. Compass; B. Radio Collar; C. Radio Antenna; D. Jab Stick; E. Scale; F. Syringe; G. Tape Measure; H. Plastic Bags; I. Ear Tag; J. Notebook; K. Airplane; L. Hand Held Command Unit

p. 25 In the Lab - 1500 raspberries seeds; 2605 hazelnuts (roughly one every 20 seconds); Bear's age - 16

p. 26 Mother is concerned about cubs - grunting; Fear - moaning, teeth-clacking; Nervous - blowing, teeth-clacking, slapping tree or ground; Terrified cub - screaming; Resting bear feeling a little tension- moaning, yawning ; Pleasure sound while nursing - motorlike noise.

p. 29 Hunting - 4, 5, 9; Poaching-2, 3,8; Accident-1,6,7

p. 30-31 Neither child is completely right. Injuries and deaths from black bears are extremely rare, but bears are wild animals and should be treated with caution and respect. Scientists who "walk with bears" have spent years studying them and are familiar with their ways.

Good: P. 30: dog on leash; bear-proof garbage can; storing food in car trunk. Upper p. 31 binoculars to watch from distance; hiking in pairs; food and garbage hanging from tree; cooking away from tent. Lower p. 31 bear bin provided for camper's food.

Bad: P. 30: open garbage can. Lower p. 31 food and sun screen on table; food in tent; cooking close to tent; garbage lying near bear bin; angler left fish on stream bank.

p. 32 1 – D; 2 – E; 3 – B; 4 – A; 5 – C

p. 36 1–Teddy Bear-D; 2–Goldilocks and the Three Bears–E; 3– Smokey Bear–A; 4–Brer Rabbit–C; 5–Big Dipper–B

p. 39 Crossword:

			S			G					P							
		P	O	L	A	R			T	O	O	T	H					
			W			I		B			A							
						Z		E			C					G		
						Z		R			H	I	G	H	W	A	Y	S
						L		R			E					R		
				D	A	Y		I			R		R			B		
				E				E			S	C	A	T		A		
		C	A	N	I	N	E	S					D			G		
		U							H				I			E		
		B	O	A	R			C	A	R	R	I	O	N				
			M						B									
			N						I			A						
		H	I	B	E	R	N	A	T	I	O	N						
			V						A			T	R	E	E			
			O				N	U	T	S		S						
S	P	I	R	I	T													
			E		A								L	I	T	T	E	R
					G													

For assistance with photos, information, inspiration, editing and critique, Dog-Eared Publications LLC thanks the following people: Dr. Lynn Rogers, Sue Mansfield, Kim Sager, Dave Manson, Maggie Heino and the work of the UW-Stevens Point Bear Research Project, Dr. Scott Craven, Dr. Jim Halfpenny, Ian McCallister, Richard Johnson, Donna Phelen, and The North American Bear Center.